Contents

Our houses

The type of house you live in may depend on the weather, the materials available to build it, or the number of people living in it.

These triangular houses in Madeira have thatched roofs. Thatch is a mixture of straw and reed.

houses
around the world

Godfrey Hall

WAYLAND

Titles in this series:
Clothes Around the World
Festivals Around the World
Food Around the World
Houses Around the World
Musical Instruments Around the World
Shops and Markets Around the World
Toys and Games Around the World
Transport Around the World

Cover pictures: (Clockwise from top) A Basotho hut village in Lesotho; an adobe house in Mali, West Africa; a slatted wooden house in Vermont, USA; a water-side wooden house on stilts in Sweden.

Contents page: Wooden houses built on stilts on the west coast of Sweden.

Series and book editor: Deb Elliott
Book design: Malcolm Walker
Cover design: Simon Balley

First published in 1995 by Wayland Publishers, Ltd, 61 Western Road, Hove, East Sussex BN3 1JD

This edition published in 1999 by Wayland Publishers Ltd

© Copyright 1995 Wayland Publishers Ltd

Find Wayland on the Internet at http://www.wayland.co.uk

British Library Cataloguing in Publication Data
Hall, Godfrey
    Houses. – (Around the World)
    I. Title II. Series
    728

ISBN 0 7502 2564 5

Typeset by Kudos Design Services, England
Printed and bound in Italy by G. Canale & C.S.p.A.

With thanks to Sue my wife, Hicham Ennami, Mike Theobald, Madeline Murphy, Joan and Harold Vidler.

Acknowledgements
The publishers would like to thank the following for allowing their pictures to be reproduced in this book: Chapel Studios 4, 13 (top); Eye Ubiquitous *Cover* (left top and bottom), 5 (top), 8, 9 (top), 13, 14, 15, 17 (bottom), 19, 20, 24, 26, 28, 29; Sally and Richard Greenhill 6 (bottom), 27(top); Robert Harding Picture Library *Cover* (top left and right), contents page, 6 (top), 8 (top), 22, 23, 27, 28 (top); Impact 10, 19 (top), 21; Rex Features 5 (bottom), 12, 16, 17 (top), 18, 25; Tony Stone Worldwide *Cover* (bottom right), 7, 9 (bottom), 11.

Some people live in flats, huts or tents. A flat is a set of rooms on one floor of a building.

In many countries, there are people without homes, who have to build shelters out of cardboard or anything else they can find.

5

Brick and stone

Bricks are rectangular blocks which have been made from clay and sand. The colour of brick houses often depends on the colour of the clay.

Many Greek houses are made of stone covered with plaster. The stone keeps the houses cool in the hot Greek climate.

This is the village of Namche Bazaar in Nepal.
The houses are made of rock and stone from the
nearby Himalaya Mountains.

Wood and mud

In countries with lots of forests, houses are often made of wood.

Here are two wooden houses on opposite sides of the world. The one on the left is in Vermont in the north-eastern USA. The one below is in South Island in New Zealand.

The house above is made of adobe, a type of clay.

The houses in the village on the right are made of mud. Mud is cheap and easy to use. It is mixed with straw to help give it strength.

Concrete and steel

Concrete is a popular material for building houses. It is made from sand, cement, stone and water. When it is mixed and allowed to dry, concrete becomes very hard.

There are so many people living in Hong Kong that there is not enough space to build houses for everyone. Instead, there are tall, concrete blocks of flats, like the ones on the left.

These modern blocks of flats in Minneapolis,
USA, are made from concrete and glass.
Steel girders are used to make the skeletons of
the tall buildings before the concrete and glass
are added.

Corrugated iron

People sometimes make their homes out of corrugated iron. This is a very cheap material which is easy to use.

The picture below shows a colourful corrugated iron house in Reykjavik, the capital of Iceland.

Many poor families who live on the edge of cities build shelters of corrugated iron. This shanty town is beside a railway station in Bombay, India.

In some countries, whole towns are built using corrugated iron for the walls and roofs of the houses. The town on the right is in Swaziland, Africa.

Kitchens

Food is usually prepared in a kitchen. In some hot countries people have open-air kitchens. They cook outside over an open fire.

Modern kitchens can have many different machines and tools for cooking and preparing food. Apart from cooking, the kitchen is also used for making drinks, storing food in cupboards and washing dishes.

Living areas

Houses often have a living area or room where families may spend time together when they are at home.

Flats in Japan are often small, so the living room may also have to be used for cooking and sleeping.

The Canadian Indians above are in the living area of their teepee.

This Swiss family are relaxing in their living room.

Sleeping areas

Sleep is good for you. In houses with only one room, it can be difficult to get a good night's sleep. At night, the family will often put up a curtain or screen. This divides the room into two.

Bedouin people live in tents which they move from place to place. Bedding has to be stored away during the day and brought out again at night. These Bedouin are from Morocco.

In countries where it can get very hot, some people prefer to sleep outside. This hammock in Peru would be very comfortable in the cool night air.

For many young people, their bedroom is a very special place where they can keep all their own things.

Protecting your house

It is important to protect your house from the weather. In very cold countries, houses have several layers of glass in the windows to keep in the heat. In warm countries, shutters are used on windows to keep out the sun so the houses stay cool.

This block of flats in London has a video camera attached which will pick up any sign of thieves.

Gardens

Gardens are places outside houses where grass, trees and flowers are often planted. The areas of grass are called lawns.

The owners of this garden have grown lots of different trees and flowers.

Most people who live in flats do not have a garden. Instead, some grow flowers in window-boxes, on balconies, or on roof terraces.

Home entertainment

Getting together at home with family and friends and enjoying yourself is important.

These friends are singing karaoke outside a house in Xining, China.

24

On hot days in many countries, children play together outside. On cold days, the house is warmer inside for playing.

Living together

Families do not always live on their own. Groups of travellers live together, moving around from one area to another.

Bedouin families also live together and move from place to place.

In Israel some families live and work on a kibbutz. They have their own set of rules and the children all live together with an adult in charge.

Something different

Houses can be built in lots of unusual ways. This house in Ho Chi Minh City in Vietnam has been built on stilts above a river.

People who like being close to water may choose to live on a houseboat.

In Cappadocia, Turkey, some people live in
hollowed-out caves in rock faces.

Glossary

Bedouin   People living in the desert areas of Jordan, Syria and Arabia who do not live in one place. Instead, they move around, packing up their tents and all their belongings and taking them to the next place.

corrugated iron   A thin sheet of iron with ridges which look like wrinkles. These ridges help to make the sheet of iron stronger.

girders Large steel beams used to build tall buildings.

hammock   A piece of canvas or netting, hung from each end and used as a comfortable place to lie down or sleep.

karaoke   A type of entertainment. People sing popular songs to background music from a machine. Sometimes there will be a television screen showing the words to the songs.

kibbutz   A place where lots of adults and children live together as one big family. Everyone shares the cooking, cleaning and care of the children.

shanty town   An area where very poor people live in shelters made from any materials they can find.

skeleton   The framework of a building before the outside materials are added.

teepee (or tepee)   A type of tent shaped like a cone.

Books to read

Materials in Your Home by Malcolm Dixon (Wayland, 1993)
Poems about Homes selected by Amanda Earl & Danielle Sensier (Wayland, 1994)
Timelines: Houses by Richard Tames (Watts, 1994)
Technology Topics: Houses and Homes by Chris Oxlade (Watts, 1994)

More information

Would you like to know more about the people and places you have seen in the photographs in this book? If so, read on.

contents page
In Sweden, houses are built of wood in areas which are close to forests. Wood is strong and long-lasting.

pages 4–5
Madeira is one of a group of volcanic islands in the North Atlantic, west of Morocco.
These flats, or apartments, are part of a block of flats in Havana, Cuba.
A homeless teenager living on the streets of London.

pages 6–7
A row of town houses in Brighton, England. The houses have been built in the Georgian style, but are very modern.
Georgian refers to the period of English history when the four Georges were kings of England – 1714 to 1830.
Plaster is a mixture of lime, sand and water, sometimes stiffened with hair or other fibres. It is applied to surfaces as a soft paste and goes very hard when dry.
Namche Bazaar is the main sherpa town in the Himalayas. In the background of the photograph looms the majestic Mount Everest.

pages 8–9
A McIndoe Falls house in Vermont, a state in the north-eastern USA. The house is in part of an area known as New England.
South Island is the largest of the islands of New Zealand. The others are North Island, Stewart Island, the Chatham Islands, and a number of minor islands in the south-east Pacific.
A traditional house in Mali, a landlocked republic in West Africa.
This is a typical Basotho hut village in Hamonaheng, Lesotho. Lesotho is a landlocked country entirely surrounded by South Africa. Basotho people are a subgroup of the Sotho people, who live mostly in Lesotho.

pages 10–11
A crowded apartment block in Hong Kong. There is a tremendous problem of overcrowding on the island. Buildings are rising higher to accomodate the growing population. In fact, the image of the Hong Kong skyline is famous throughout the world.
A futuristic-looking apartment block in downtown Minneapolis, Minnesota in the USA. The buildings are made of concrete and glass giving panoramic views of the northern American city.

pages 12–13
The island republic of Iceland contains large areas of glaciers, snowfields and lava beds with many volcanoes and hot springs. The island's power comes mainly from natural sources – the hot springs provide geothermal energy.
This shanty town is beside the railway line at Bandra station in Bombay, India. Homelessness is a serious problem in India. Many millions of people live on the streets, well below the poverty line.
This town in Swaziland was built specially to house the temporary workers and their families who come to work in the nearby mines. Swaziland is an area in South Africa.

pages 14–15
A family after their evening meal in the open air in Namibia, in south-west Africa.
These three American teenagers are making a salad in their kitchen.

pages 16–17
Traditionally, Japanese homes have limited furnishing – known as minimalist.
A teepee, or tepee, is a cone-shaped tent made from animal skins.
The living room of a house in Lausanne, Switzerland.

page 18–19
The Bedouin are people who live in the deserts of Arabia, Jordan and Syria. Bedouin do not have one place they call home. Instead they choose to move from place to place, packing up their tents and belongings each time.
A hammock is a length of canvas or net, suspended at the ends and used as a bed. This hammock is in a town near Iquitos, a port in north-east Peru.
Children playing the game of Trivial Pursuit in their bedroom in Spain.

pages 20–21
Shutters are hinged door-like covers, often louvred, which open and close a window. Shutters are more common in hot countries, since they keep rooms and buildings cool.
A security camera used to prevent burglars at a block of flats in Southwark, London.

pages 22–23
A country garden in Eastnor in the county of Hereford and Worcestershire, England.
A window-box in the Italian city of Venice.

pages 24–25
Karaoke is a popular form of entertainment all over the world. People have to sing well-known songs to accompany a machine which plays background music and shows the lyrics of the songs.
Children outside their home in a village in Kampuchea (formerly known as Cambodia).

pages 26–27
Travelling people inside their caravan home in Wales.
A Bedouin village by the Red Sea, which runs between Arabia and north-east Africa.
A kibbutz is a settlement in Israel where people all live together sharing duties and growing their own food. Care of the children is taken by all the adults and not just by the children's parents.

pages 28–29
Stilts are a pair of long poles used to support a building above ground or water level. This house on stilts in Vietnam is above the Rach Thi Nghe, a backwater of the Saigon River.
Houseboats on the River Nile in India.
Cappadocia is an ancient region in Turkey.

Index

Curriculum Visions

Where we live

PLACES/SETTLEMENT

SECOND EDITION

Dr Brian Knapp

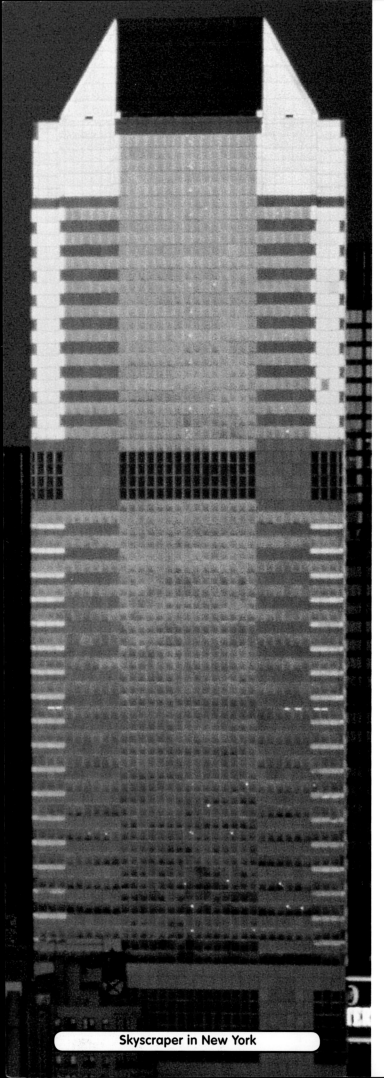

Skyscraper in New York

Curriculum Visions

There's more online

See our great collection of page-turning books and multimedia resources at:

www.CurriculumVisions.com

(CurriculumVisions is a subscription web site)

This second edition © Atlantic Europe Publishing 2011

First edition 1999. First reprint 2003. Second reprint 2005. Second edition 2011.

The right of Brian Knapp to be identified as the author of this work has been asserted by him in accordance with the Copyright, Designs and Patents Act 1988.

Author
Brian Knapp, BSc, PhD

Senior Designer
Adele Humphries, BA, PGCE

Editor
Gillian Gatehouse

Designed and produced by
Atlantic Europe Publishing

Printed in China by
WKT Company Ltd

Where we live (Places/Settlement) 2nd edition – Curriculum Visions
A CIP record for this book is available from the British Library

Paperback ISBN 978 1 86214 683 9

Picture credits
All photographs are from the ShutterStock and Earthscape Picture Libraries except the following: (c=centre t=top b=bottom l=left r=right)
FEMA page 20tl, *Leeds City Libraries* page 42, *The Stock Market* page 18, *University of Reading, Rural History Centre* pages 8, 43t.
The publishers have made their best endeavours to contact all copyright holders for material published in this book.

This product is manufactured from sustainable managed forests. For every tree cut down at least one more is planted.